ANIMAL LIFE STORIES

THE FROG

Published by Warwick Press,
387 Park Avenue South, New York, N.Y. 10016.
First published in this edition by
Kingfisher Books, 1989. Some of the illustrations
in this book are taken from the First Look
at Nature series.

6 5 4 3 2 1

Printed in Spain

Library of Congress Catalog Card No. 89-50005
ISBN 0-531-19058-7

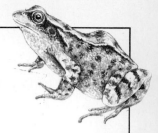

ANIMAL LIFE STORIES

THE FROG

By Angela Royston
Illustrated by Bernard Robinson

Warwick Press
New York/London/Toronto/Sydney
1989

It is spring and the female frog is fat and heavy with eggs. She hears the male frogs at the pond calling the females to mate. As she slowly hops toward them, the croaking gets louder and louder.

She reaches the pond and slides into the water. A male frog grips her closely, and they swim together for a whole day and a night.

When morning comes the female pushes with her
legs, and all her eggs flow into the water. The male
frog squirts his sperm over the eggs.

The female is now as thin as the male, and she is very tired. She climbs up onto the bank and looks around for a place to rest.

She snaps up a juicy snail, then creeps into a damp
hollow under a stone. She does not even see the newt
slithering past her, and soon she is fast asleep.

Thick blobs of jelly swell around the eggs and sperm, and the pond is soon full of floating spawn. Fish and ducks nibble away at some of it, but inside the rest of the spawn small black specks are growing into tadpoles.

Two.weeks later, the tadpoles begin to hatch. They cling to the water weeds and swim with their wriggling tails. But they are still not safe from the fish or the sharp beak of a heron.

The tadpoles feed on tiny water plants and grow larger each day. When they are six weeks old they start to change shape.

First back legs and then front legs push through a fold of skin. Their mouths become stronger so they can eat worms and insects. Soon their lungs develop so they can breathe in air as well as in water, and when they are eleven weeks old they are ready to leave the pond.

One warm summer's afternoon the little frogs
wriggle out of their tight tadpole skins and hop onto
dry land. They gaze around them with bulging
eyes. There are lots of insects to eat now. A large
frog sitting nearby shoots out her sticky tongue and
catches a dragonfly.

But the frogs are not the only ones who are hungry.
A grass snake slithers toward the big frog. She
hears it rustling and with a huge leap jumps away
just in time.

The young frogs are only as big as a thumbnail, and many of them are pounced on by hedgehogs, birds, and rats. The others soon learn to stay safely hidden.

Summer soon turns to fall and the frogs have grown much bigger. As the days get colder the frogs find there is not much food for them to eat, and it is too cold to move about.

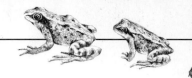

One by one they each find a hole at the bottom of the pond or around its sides. Here they will sleep throughout the winter, safe from enemies and the cold snow and ice.

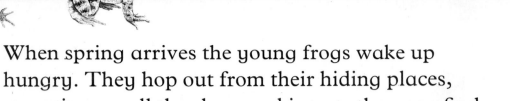

When spring arrives the young frogs wake up hungry. They hop out from their hiding places, snapping up all the slugs and insects they can find.

The adult frogs are all waking up too. The large males are croaking by the pond again, and the females, fat with eggs, are hopping toward them. But it will be two more years before the young frogs have grown big enough to join them.

More about Frogs

There are many kinds of frogs in the world. The frog in this story is the common frog, which lives in America and Europe and the cooler parts of Asia.

Edible frog
from America
and Europe

Marsh frog
from Europe

Reed frog
from Africa

Tree frog
from Australia

All frogs croak by pushing air backward and forward over their throats. Some, like the reed frog and the edible frog, have flaps of loose skin which they blow up into bubbles to make the sound louder. A frog's skin is so thin water can pass through it. Frogs have to keep their skin damp so they don't dry out. Tree frogs live in warm wet jungles and use the puddles which form in the large leaves.

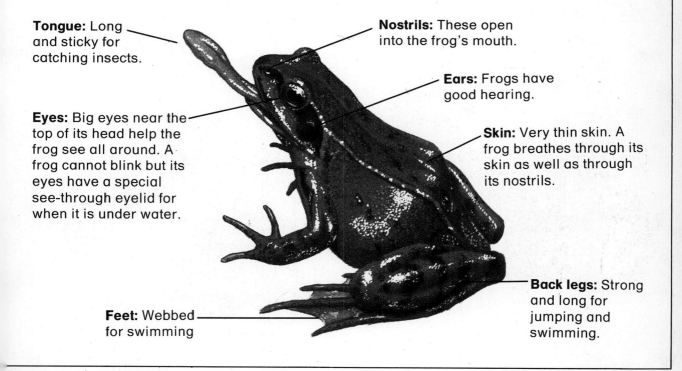

Tongue: Long and sticky for catching insects.

Nostrils: These open into the frog's mouth.

Ears: Frogs have good hearing.

Eyes: Big eyes near the top of its head help the frog see all around. A frog cannot blink but its eyes have a special see-through eyelid for when it is under water.

Skin: Very thin skin. A frog breathes through its skin as well as through its nostrils.

Back legs: Strong and long for jumping and swimming.

Feet: Webbed for swimming

Some Special Words

Amphibian An animal which can live both in water and on land. Frogs begin life as tadpoles, then change into frogs and move onto the land.

Dragonfly A large insect with a long body and two sets of wings.

Grass snake This grayish-green snake lives in damp places and swims well. It is harmless to people but eats frogs and toads.

Heron A large gray and white bird with long legs. It feeds on fish and other water animals.

Newt This animal looks rather like a lizard but is an amphibian.

Spawn A jelly-like mass of frog's eggs growing into tadpoles.

Sperm Male seed which joins with an egg from the female and grows into a new life.